I0155378

Earthen

poems by

Thomas Festa

Finishing Line Press
Georgetown, Kentucky

Earthen

For Joann Deiudicibus

ACKNOWLEDGMENTS

Much gratitude to the editors of the following publications, in which some of
these poems first appeared, some in earlier form:

Bennington Review: "The Sculpted Radiance of What Remained"
Chronogram: "Andalusian June," "On a Distant Prospect of the Zen
    Mountain Monastery," "Snowbound, Evening Light"
Haiku Journal: "Kyoto-Paris" (i) and (ii)
Lightwood Magazine: "The Algebra of Origins," "On the Death of Miles
    Davis"
Poetry Quarterly: "Field Trip," "Switchback"
Shawangunk Review: "Cover of Time," "Incompleteness Theorem," "Renga
    of the Self"

Heartfelt thanks to friends who offered incisive comments and encouraging
words on poems in progress: Claire Hero, Glenn Lyvers, Jed Mayer,
Jon Munk, Phillip X. Levine, Jan Zlotnik Schmidt, and the late Pauline
Uchmanowicz. Laurence (Larry) Carr deserves a sentence all to himself for
his friendship and support. The dedication records my deepest debt.

Publisher: Leah Huete de Maines
Editor: Christen Kincaid
Cover Art: Dietmar Rabich / Wikimedia Commons / "Dülmen, Kirchspiel,
    Börnste, Abstrakte Bäume—2021—8241" / CC BY-SA 4.0
Author Photo: Mike McGregor, https://mikemcgregor.com
Cover Design: Elizabeth Maines McCleavy

Order online: www.finishinglinepress.com
        also available on amazon.com

Author inquiries and mail orders:
Finishing Line Press
PO Box 1626
Georgetown, Kentucky 40324
USA

Table of Contents

Andalusian June..........1

The Sculpted Radiance of What Remained..........2

Incompleteness Theorem..........3

On the Death of Miles Davis..........5

On a Distant Prospect of the Zen Mountain Monastery..........7

The Algebra of Origins..........8

Field Trip..........9

Travelogue..........11

Cover of Time..........12

The Motion Picture Hospital..........13

Catalogue of Ships..........14

Rowing to Innisfallen..........15

Switchback..........16

Snowbound, Evening Light..........17

He Grieved Fluently in Seven Languages..........18

When We Know Our Names..........20

Kyoto-Paris..........21

Renga of the Self..........22

Peregrine Question..........23

Illuminated Manuscript..........24

Words for _____..........25

Etymology of Need..........26

You of All..........27

That There Could Be Such Brightness in the World..........28

earthen, adj.
"*Characteristic of or situated on the earth as opposed to heaven;*
merely material; mundane, worldly. Now rare."
—*Oxford English Dictionary, definition 4*

Andalusian June
(In memoriam Pauline Uchmanowicz)

Bare feet flat on earthen tiles,
cool soles pat arabesques.
It's solstice. Out tall window-doors,
spires to remind us
of what we'll never be, reach…

The sound of distant river's
unmistakable, smacks
of wine spilled for you, water,
friend, close by, a windswept
fountain heard as laughing patios of praise.

So like solace in this year of loss,
the missed rising to the longest sun.

Evanescent minds are minarets of grief,
break silence nebulous as clouds,
literal as belief,

when we ignore the call to prayer
trilling against that tendered sky,
roseate
twilight of pursed lips—

this is how I remember losing…

The Sculpted Radiance of What Remained

I think of my student who couldn't speak
and run out of myths to pack

for the journey. We say *spectrum*—
as if the quest begun were an exile's homecoming.

He made no eye contact, no sound except when,
overtaken by connections

no one else could see, he'd cross an ocean
of restless imagination

and clap once, a barred owl's wingbeat
at midday. He pecked out his papers, typing

with one index finger for a stretch of twelve hours,
elaborating ornate allegories, glass towers

moated with blood. Awful grace molten out of pain.
I follow the owl down the rail trail to its carrion

feast, knowing myself an uninvited guest.
A one-armed woman walks past

my window each morning,
gives a shy wave when she sees me looking.

I teach like our fates depended on this wave, gesture
of welcome or departure.

My heart and head of ash
remember how at that last class he shook my hand.

Incompleteness Theorem

Ethiopia meant two things:
low birthweight, Greek for *burned face.*

Ash, there are moments when
the whole world closes in on itself,
some wicked proof or dying ember.
Angels of defilement scrape
the sky clean. Paint-by-numbers

shows through imperfectly
like stained glass social workers

made your folks replace.
The agency said too much lead
to let in baby you.

Now, as you ready yourself
for another change of address,

pencil marks on a bedroom
doorframe painted over
reveal growth measured
as loss. How dare I

call this haven, Ash, this sanctuary
home, you twice unmothered,
this far from Africa, answerable
questions, feasts
for vacationing gods?

Love, like any name,
is adopted—nectar of mooring
nurture. Your visage flames
darkest roses. How hard you tried
to express nothing, the face
of having nothing to say.

Where does the emptiness
come from, knowing
there's nothing but illusion
with which one fills the void.

On the Death of Miles Davis

In the hospital where I was born, St. John's
in Santa Monica, my grandmother cared for Miles Davis
till they turned the machine off
and he breathed his last breath.

Before that, his breath and I
had only ever been connected by machines,
acquainted by vinyl and silkscreen:
my father's abandoned record
collection, *Kind of Blue* and *Sketches of Spain*;
and concert t-shirts
for the *Tutu* and *Amandla* tours
I helped Keith make at work.
                                        She told
of the ravages he suffered, singular at the end
as he had been from the start, mightily
protesting himself into a coma.
                                        It is not
the tone of another world, but this one,
cussed and sutured so to heal,
scars within earshot. Not turning away
from the audience, as in later years onstage,
but outburst from a backlit thunderhead.

                                        She mentioned
flowers, followers,
hangers on,
ambivalences of family,
all peeled away, dropped
like petals
into municipal water
in a glass vase.

                                                    I can't believe
Bitches Brew
is as old as I am.
What drove my grandmother's years of volunteering
comes to me like forgotten names of constellations.
Feline, lithe in your approach, we have hardly made you out
in the night sky, nor can we glean your shape,
a breath through innermost brightness, the bell
of that last trumpet. Another, tolling.
Each one of us listening, sounding
the syncopated notes of our own desolation.

On a Distant Prospect of the Zen Mountain Monastery

I speed past you, silent one,
admire your far-off gaze tranquil as a sky lake,

and long for order in the jaws of desire
as the kids scream in the back seat.

The Algebra of Origins

Algebra, Latin for computation;
surgical treatment of fractures;
derived from Arabic, *al-jabr*,
the restoration of anything missing, lost,
out of place, lacking;
the reunion of broken parts.

On the school playground,
my daughter broke the birdlike bones
of her left arm.

In a sudden downpour, a tree
falls out of common usage,
split low on the trunk.

The forest remembers dead languages,
the radius and ulna, forgotten paths.

She didn't cry her whole time in Emergency.
Shock retold each new face the jagged tale,
how she broke her fall.

My little daughter's bones
set in sleep and draped in fiberglass
begin to heal.

She discovers the aftermath below
the poplar that struck our deck,
dead swallows in a birdhouse on the ground.

As we flew down the highway
to the hospital where she was born,
her suffering stole all meaning from my words,
but on my face I could feel
the shadows of a vast flock
passing in silent unison overhead.

Field Trip

Waves of stone rise ahead,
swells in an earthen ocean.
On the mountainside, early
morning, mid-October.
Mist rises from the valley
floor, the glint of river
scything through. The air
is thinner, it gets harder to
lie to yourself, on the ridge.
Slopes look gentler from afar
than up close, sheer crags
and scree, surge of shale
and graywacke sandstone, bedrock
lifted up and warped
in the Permian. These breakers, too,
someday will crash.
They image permanence

for now, like the group
shot we'll snap at the peak.
Classmates you'd rather play
with won't matter in
a dozen years, but they're
as important as you think

for now. Dense geologic
folds—synclines, anticlines—
dot the horizon like
opposed fates you could choose.

To own your homing you
must listen, not to me
walking near, but to
the silent expanse beyond
that vanishing point. And so
we hike together, Son,
for this brief time, this being
all we have. For now

we breathe hard together,
remember, it is glorious.

Travelogue

Often we set out but didn't reach the islands.
Santa Cruz and Anacapa'd grow up
as if anticipating our arrival.
Outboard off, we'd tack, not talk, inured
to words, jib the genny when he'd yell,
relieved to find a footing where no tact
was called for. No doubt you've heard the one about
the man who sees his father for the first
time under ice, frozen younger than
the son discovering his patrimony?
At fifty, I realize my dad, then forty,
organized the failure of those trips
so we would have to turn back disappointed,
sail through the first darkness, home.

Cover of Time

The blind thrust earthquake killed my mother's classroom aide's son and husband in their beds, Northridge tenement stucco stories crushed together under a covering of dust. Angela. She was from Manila, *nila* from Sanskrit for indigo tree, or flowering mangrove. Her face on the cover of *Time* did not belong—no more belonging left, only suffering, the universe made self-aware in pain. We all feared aftershocks, the fault. Our own condemned, we had to move while foundations repaired and walls shored up against the next vibration, the viola in California, the quiver of the angelus. Across town, in a nearly identical apartment, removed from habits and glances, learning to ignore notions like providence, homecoming, and biding my time. Blue quietude descended, as unforeknown as the angel of a furious annunciation, a lake without ripples shimmering, paper napkins blown in a gust. A whisper (not in parentheses) from the great blank outside, a spoor newly scented on the arid wind of ethics. The flowers are small, bell-shaped, blossom in late summer or early autumn. They're blue, or red, the kind everyone recognizes but no one can name.

The Motion Picture Hospital

Wherever you were in F-ward,
you could hear the ancient voice.
In that bleached-out, reeking, stainless-steel place
where forgotten child actors went to die,
I delivered pureed splat on trays,
heart fat, ears heavy, in my B movie
suburb of L.A. The old lady cried out,
not a question, Can you hear me;
pleading, pitch rising, Can you help me?
Gringo green, age fifteen,
I entered the room, stared into the milked abyss
of her blind eyes, and answered her.
And saw out the window like a movie screen
crows seeking asylum in a lonely sycamore,
plastic bags blowing in an abandoned lot, and, overlaid,
trails of mascara down a slack, blank face.
Can you see me—
she droned on like this every day,
though I couldn't have known
when first I crossed that threshold,
entered her room, and lied yes,
and she, staring at nothing with such ferocity and terror,
cried—Can you help me, God?—
a silent movie's onetime star.

Catalogue of Ships

That boring passage you can't bear to reread
has something vital to tell you about life.
Admit that it's not what you thought at first,
not a lifelike toy to take or leave,
but life itself. Admit defeat
before it: trips to the shore
that failed to keep your marriage
from collapse, stays at the hospital
that didn't cure you, the damage handed on
to your children unawares. Admit
you do care before you sail past
false starts and good intentions,
the childhood operations.
It's not what you thought,
not about what you thought,
always wanting something else
—more sex, more sense, more sums—
desire like a simile
that lies about the quantities of life.
Who's first, who's last?—a stitch tucked in the weave
of need. Archaic tales confirm
the circling ocean of suspicion,
that the war was not about lost love
and the rage that moved the gods would also pass.

Rowing to Innisfallen

What else but ruins
did the guidebook promise?
Sika deer, foxgloves in flower,
the sun lifejacket orange behind
stained monastic stones…

We crossed the Lake of Learning
in a listing boat,
each under the cowl
of our own dark ages.

Counterweight unshifted,
we drifted through the apocalypse
till the graves yawned awake
and marriage ended, or began

to. Silent, the deer swam by,
climbed to shore before us
like lepers, monks, high kings
—not an unrecoverable dream,
but the childhood of familiar things.

Ripples from cardinal directions
galloped against the stern,
miniature horsemen
of the compass rose.

Switchback

I imagine we walk together,
a childless hike on the ridge.
The crisp new air clarifies
more than views or destinations.
No reply could correspond
to felt need. There have been
these many years. In the air,
a taint of seasons turned,
withdrawals unbeknownst.
When we speak of impracticality
talk is never intimate, longing
forgotten. But the scent
rides on the air, pine resin
and sawdust, fallen trees cleared.

Snowbound, Evening Light

We have been here all along,
so it will occur to us
on the other side
when we reach out our fingertips like leaves
for the last light,
laughing,
we have never been.

He Grieved Fluently in Seven Languages

—Urdu, Hebrew, Arabic, Amharic, Malay, Latin,
and native
English—

but refused his own funeral.
Said we couldn't grieve for another,
only ourselves. Lion cubs

learn to hunt with fake prey.
Yet again to mourn him I
inhale; the attempt

catches. Lungs and throat
lurch. Uphill, at the end
of the breath,

a stone oak grows beside
the rushes of a flower rinsing creek
and a thatched hut.

Another breath fills my lungs
like his cancer, like fluency
in a dead language.

A secret dwelling, nearly unreal,
like shame
at having been born

with cerebral palsy. Shining
lair. All the clowning
could never disguise

the lazy eye, the sober slur,
the twin given up at thirteen.
His loss made breathing

feel like clumsiness.
A spasm of kinship
shabbily concealed,

like the eyeshine
of a hiding cat
in the full moon newly risen.

When We Know Our Names

Downed powerlines slip through slick palms, explanation and doubt carving lifelines into unsuspecting hands. Who knew that we, fieldhands in a brushfire, held power? Still the headlands burn, now *become* wildfire. Chaparral's disappearing. We're all familiar with this ice plant covered peninsula, mudflats and barrens alongside the expressway. Conveyed from the Cape of Good Hope to stabilize the soil, ice plant crawls waterward, augurs eroding coasts. The wind blows where it lists, and you hear its sound but can't tell where it comes from, where it goes. We live at the wind's address, embalmed in honey and called after different saints, not to be confused with Father. Rabbi, he said, rabbi, I'm allergic to wild honey and locusts, though the son of an entomologist. We are inmates of the same asylum, though I belong to the river community, and you, you hit the rock and hit the rock again, an omen heard inert, water silenced. A white-robed goddess saunters across the distant green fields. Her voice melds with the wind; she sluices down as rain; she only knows me by my middle name. Waiting for inhibition of return, I mean reuptake, I have to check my blood level. It's a bleaching coral reef, our history, written across tide pools in colors found only in dreams, a riot of sea anemones.

Kyoto-Paris

i.

Rotten timber deck
      sparrow's nest under rafters
            all we wait for comes

ii.

Amber leaves shudder
      a thieving hand of bright wind
            picking death's pocket

iii.

Then they found the sheen
      you could not drink the water
            spring without rebirth

iv.

No seasonal word
      will do—May snow on white birch
            accords with torn flesh

Renga of the Self

The patter of rain
on the roof this not-yet-spring
past the equinox

upstate swings, selfish.
Foot-tap invocations, brief
shows of gratitude

too early or too
late arrive febrile, ready
to grow. Things not said

interspersed with sobs
from the antique library
table and matching

desk reach rooms across
the continent scattered with
the half-packed boxes

of inheritance.
Among the fading photos
in the album I

found from the start of
the last century: one of
the old house downtown

I never entered,
of the living room, by chance
authenticates the

antiquity and
formal essence, the
tableness of the table.

Peregrine Question

An answer lies among the dark brushwork,
calligraphy of the leafless poplars
in the wind. The raccoon's curved carcass poses
no question. What quandary the turn

of the dry ravine, or tart, barbed curl
of the wineberry shoot? How to get by rote
the hierophant markings of the algal blooms
greening the inkpot pond? Stranger,

thorn flower and thistle syntactically arrange
your dominion in a sentence no
convict wants to hear. But all below
await the verdict of beak and talon,

the revelation of your lethal grace.
You spread your throne in middle air
as if at the world's last session
and plunge toward the work of judgment

devouring every flutter of doubt.
Alien flowering, true north of curiosity,
my nib's hooded, my head bowed.
Yours are scriptures we could never write

much less learn to read with the conscious mind,
should it exist. At your cry, I look up,
glimpse only your vanishing motion,
and hear the flex of hollow bones in flight.

Illuminated Manuscript

About the book I want to give you,
a vellum devotional, and why I hesitate,
not out of fear of you, but of myself:

my imagination of your imagination;
what your reaction could provoke in me,
all it might entail…Distrusting metaphysics,

you rightly argue that these stories, though true,
aren't contained in the text—
mere marginalia. Yet their ache glows toward you,

their breath on the back of your neck.
A first brush of lips and tongue. A moistened finger
paging through the Book of Hours

to find your initials inked in oak gall and ash
on pumice-smoothed skin. Just devotion
in a scriptorium near the cloisters, rigors

of a hedge maze drawn. The artificer's passion,
incipit wreathed in ornamenting pain,
flush against yours, binds us as codex together.

Words for _____

I write these words so you might hear them
as if in your own voice—writing of you
till it makes something happen.
As if anticipation could produce
melody for an unheard song,
though strangers keep wandering into the room
playing their unstrung instruments loudly, loudly.
As if you left me stranded, alone in a remote
country where I don't know the language
or customs of greeting. As if all song began
in fire and ended in utterance of your name,
and the short interval between
if and *flame* were a flint struck
in a ritual we are yet to invent.

Etymology of Need

You sleep, your face in calm repose
beyond me. Pangs sharpen this morning
to needle tips of need.
What it would be, then,
would be a way
to cast off sorrow and sighing,
the rust inside of trust.
Is this what it means: not to know,
but, awake, to yearn toward
recumbent desire, your wind knocked right out?
For beauty catches as breath catches—
no pleasure without danger.
Within this promise, miming assurance
but uncertainly,
the thrum and whirr of helicopter
seeds repeats,
you the Norway maple
afire in fall,
I the winged
samara tottering on the seam
of unclean rain gutters, waiting for more wind.
A waterfall frozen mid-
plunge. Spun aloft in your catchment,
drifting down dark currents of need,
dream knowing
what I cannot,
why anyone should grieve
the conceivable ground
beyond possession,
the life beyond
this fatal, vertiginous drop,
infinitely-many infinities
just out of reach.

You of All

Against a backdrop of paths through tall grass in sun showers,
the mountain ridge falling away into the day's last light,
and the ring of footfalls echoing down
the corridor of a mental ward; against
chance and probability, ends and odds
calculated or imagined; against hope and others' judgments:
I choose you.

As a charm against foreboding, doom, and predicted failure;
fragrant against reason, scents,
and rhyme, memory and forgetting, time,
eternity, and whatever's in between; as talisman
to ward off insomnia and nightmare;
against exes and hexes, faith and disbelief:
I choose you.

Against the grain and the grape, beyond fear and confidence,
are the words you gave me
braiding together to form an oath
knotted by the mind against time;
against myself questing toward you, up against
the world, or you, finding and binding a new self each time
you choose me.

That There Could Be Such Brightness in the World

When you asked
if we could wander the cemetery grounds,

it brought back
our first touch—

how in the funeral home foyer, we hugged
as if all love began in loss.

At tombstones' smooth-worn thresholds,
autumn means increase, destruction.

Light-struck, the angel's face
featureless, gone to an even, misty gray.

Still, observe
the posture of oblation, the will of stone.

Today's spring equinox.
After winter's longest-shortest month,

day once again equals night.
Here's not a painter's precision of blueness, no

tube of cerulean, ultramarine, or cobalt,
but unbroken sky above

skulls lodged in arroyo mud,
incised reminders, scattered offerings

of odd memorials: faded baseball caps,
mute ukuleles, empty Guinness bottles,

whatever scraps of recollection
might be left to stand in for what meant.

You, brightness, are a world
unto yourself. In this séance

of the senses, I listen,
hand in disbelieving hand.

For this duration, your light
before me, even I can withstand

such reverence
and the silence after.

Thomas Festa is Professor of English at the State University of New York, New Paltz. Born in Santa Monica, California, he graduated summa cum laude from UCLA and holds a Ph.D. from Columbia University. He is the author of a study of John Milton's poetry, *The End of Learning* (2006), as well as over two dozen scholarly articles, and has co-edited four anthologies, including the award-winning feminist teaching text, *Early Modern Women on the Fall* (2012). His poems have appeared in *Bennington Review, Chronogram, Haiku Journal, Lightwood Magazine, Poetry Quarterly, Shawangunk Review,* and elsewhere.